Ecology II:
Throat Song from the Everglades

Ecology II:
Throat Song from the Everglades

Poems by Anne McCrary Sullivan

WordTech Editions

Published by WordTech Editions
P.O. Box 541106
Cincinnati, OH 45254-1106

ISBN: 9781934999462
LCCN: 2009921052

Poetry Editor: Kevin Walzer
Business Editor: Lori Jareo

Cover design: Kristi Donahue
Cover photography: Brian F. Call

Visit us on the web at www.wordtechweb.com

Acknowledgments

I appreciate that several of these poems first appeared elsewhere:

Land Views: Online Journal of Landscape, Art, and Design —"Rangers of the Everglades" and "El Laguno del Espiritu Santo"
Tar River Poetry—"Mother Collecting Marine Specimens" and "Mother in Water"
Fourth River—"Lobelia"
The Gettysburg Review—"Notes from a Marine Biologist's Daughter"
The Southern Review—"I Came to tahe Everglades with a Grief," "Holding On," and "Anhinga Pairing"

I would like to thank publications where some of these poems have been re-published: "Notes from a Marine Biologist's Daughter," "Mother Collecting Marine Specimens" and "Mother in Water" have appeared within the context of an article in *Harvard Educational Review*. "Notes from a Marine Biologist's Daughter" was selected for *Choice Magazine Listening*. "Holding On" and "Anhinga Pairing" were featured on *Verse Daily*.

Every book has a peopled history and many influences. This one certainly would not have come into being without the opportunity to live in the Everglades for a time as a guest of the Artists in Residence in the Everglades (AIRIE) program. I am deeply grateful for the rangers of Everglades National Park who have been my guides and teachers, especially those who first introduced me to a sawgrass world and those who have continued to support my work over a period of several years —Maureen Ballinger-McGee, Alan Scott, Cherry Payne, Jackie Destourian, Sandy Dayhoff, Frankie Aranzamendi, and Bob Merkle. A special thanks to Donna Marxer, whose inspiration and efforts led to the creation of the AIRIE program.

The influence of the Warren Wilson MFA Program for Writers has been inestimable. Profound thanks to my supervising teachers Joan Aleshire, Marianne Boruch, Ira Sadoff, and Michael Collier; and also to John Skoyles, Greg Orr and Ellen Bryant Voigt whose influences have been substantial.

The ongoing community of Warren Wilson Alumni has supported and sustained me with friendship and critique. Easy satisfaction has not been an option. Special thanks to the outrageous Terri Ford who has helped me to unlearn timidity; to Martha Carlson-Bradley who would not give up her urging; and to the grand sisterhood of manuscript scrutiny.

In my academic world, I have enjoyed the energetic support of colleagues at National-Louis University and of the Dean, Alison Hilsabeck, who regularly reads poems to us at faculty meetings. My colleagues in the Arts-Based Educational Research SIG of the American Educational Research Association and at the National Council of Teachers of English have also been important. Ben Nelms and Rob Sherman have played crucial roles in supporting my work.

A few long-term friends stand out, each having made a unique and important contribution as support and/or catalyst: Holly Genzen, Joanna Michaels, Randy DelLago, Michelle Commeyras.

And underlying everything, the heartbeat of family—my sons, Kenyata and Jolyon; my amazing daughters-in-law Grace and Linda; grandchildren Miller, Bremen, Grace and Anne Elizabeth; my one and only phenomenal niece, Rachael; a host of cousins who have been more important than they know; and Dovie, grandmother who taught me fierce unconditional love.

The work of this book has been supported by an Artist Professional Development Grant from the Pinellas County Arts Council (Florida); by residencies at the Hambidge Center for Creative Arts and Sciences (Georgia), the Weymouth Center (North Carolina), Big Cypress National Preserve (Florida) and the South Carolina State Parks Artists-in-Residence program; by a sabbatical from National-Louis University; and by Karen.

It takes a village to make a book. Thank you.

For my mother, Anne Bowden McCrary,
marine biologist who taught me by example
to see, name, and love the world

and

for my brother, Everett,
who lives on the edge of a volcano
and hears the wind before it comes.

Table of Contents

Let my heart be feral.
—Mary Kay Rummel

Orientation

If you leave
the door
       open

and a pygmy
rattler
       gets in

just get
a broom

and sweep
her out

       gently.

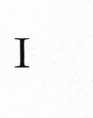

Holding On

I'm thinking of them tonight, locked in their embrace,
waters dark and cold. Do they have any warmth
to give each other? Late yesterday, near exhaustion,
they lay in the slough overhung with reed and pond apple,
motionless—gator's jaws clamped onto the python's thick
muscle, python wrapped around the gator's rough trunk.
It started early, morning light slicing water. The python
coiled and writhed, head waving above the fight. The gator
wrestled, then backed from the slough, submerged and swam
through open water—a gator drowns its prey—
but when he surfaced, the python's head lifted, stared him in the eye.
All day it went like that, slough to slough, diving and surfacing,
python wrapped around the gator's snout, then a lurch,
python in the gator's mouth but the head
still lifting. What respect they must have for each other by now.
Neither lets go. Neither is winning. They aren't even fighting.
They lie in the dark and hold on.

Anhinga Pairing

When the male anhinga's bright blue eye ring comes,
when he displays his fine feathers, raising his tail,
waving the wings, she begins to pay attention.
Then they swoop and glide together
near the nesting area—preen together, lifting
and fluffing feathers, rubbing each other's bills.
But they are not a pair until he finds the perfect
twig, offers it to her and she accepts.

Last year we saw him offer a twig, and she took it.
Even as we were all saying "Ahhh..." she lifted
that stick and hit him in the head with it, flew away.

Acceptance means something. And when she does
accept, they become *monogamous in a bond that lasts
several years.* What I haven't been able to learn
is how they go about separation. Is it mutual, a sort of inherent
biological timing? Or does one just leave? And for the other,
is there grief?

Protected: The Pied-billed Grebe

See how she alters her own specific gravity,
bobs on the surface then submerges,
swims long underwater, safe, invisible?

She gulps down jointed bodies of crayfish,
armored beetles, bony fish, then swallows
the protection of her own molted feathers.

Her stomach churns with soft and sharp
till all that is hard and indigestible
rises, floats, a down-tufted ball.

When her chicks are newly hatched,
they leave the nest, climb onto her, tuck
themselves between the wing and ...

grebe-fur they called it, those 19th century hunters
and milliners, skin with thick insulating
feathers, perfect for coats and capes.

Coontie: *zamia pumilla*

Burn everything that's green,
every part of it that looks alive,
it comes back lush—delicate
fronds arching from a stub of root.

Zamia means *hurt.* These ancient cycads,
experts in damage, shared the Earth
with dinosaurs, hoarded starch
in underground stems, survived.

That starch is deadly but the natives learned
(how did they do that? how many died?)
to leach the poison—boil, pound, grind,
lay it in the sun to dry,

make meal for steaming bowls of sofkee,
good sweet loaves of bread.

I Came to the Everglades with a Grief

This is what I have learned: weeping for beauty
replaces weeping for grief. Stunned at first
by the blue heron's crest, the purple gallinule's
iridescence, grief now creeps as surely forward
as this subtle river of grass flows south.

It goes about its quiet work stealthy
as the yellow panther in the understory,
necessary, as everything here is necessary
each to the other in a complex ecology.

Yesterday, only once I felt it moving. It lifted
like a bird from the expanse of sawgrass,
startled me. I had stopped looking for it.

This grief is learning to ride the anhinga, glide
and flap through forgiving air. It lands in bark-stained
water, dives beneath the surface, swims—I see it there,
indistinct shape, a quivering blur. On the bank,

the gator's black back stretched in sun
amazes me, makes me think that I can touch
a fine living leather with claws and teeth.

The Drydown

A year's rains have fallen. Water drains through limestone
into aquifers. Prairies dry.
At diminishing sloughs, solitary creatures congregate—
fin, fur and leather.

For water birds it is a rich time, fish of a thousand acres
swimming in a narrow stream.
The ibis probes, the spoonbill scythes, the pink-footed
wood stork stirs marl.

It is a time for nesting, an abundance of food for the young.
And some of the young
will *be* food. And some of the parents will be food. And no,
this is not a tragedy.

In sawgrass and marl the gator swings his tail, thrashes out
a damp domain
where birds, raccoon and panther come. He is lord of the truce
and its inevitable breach.

Drawn to his pool, I invent my hymns of praise and healing,
lift a fragrant bitterness
to my tongue, remind myself: it is only a season. Only a season.
The rains will come.

II

10-Month-Old Road-Killed Florida Panther
—After Brian Call's photograph

Precisely at the center of the dark road
forming a cross with the white line,
the broken panther lies, its mouth
spilling blood. At first I couldn't look,
but I've come back to see

how gently it lies on the pavement, stretched
on its side, tail extended—how easy it would be
to stroke its shadowed fur. I wonder—

Did the photographer do that?
Did he place his hand on the cat's head,
rub a little between the ears, follow
with his hand the curve of the neck,
the long back, the soft haunch?
And did he do this before
or after he took the photograph—blood
still pooling, fur still warm.

Train in the Tropics

Air motionless, muggy in my room, I got up,
turned on the ceiling fan, lay back down to its irritating
rhythmic groan, told myself this is just another sound
of the tropics—another frog, another cricket. It didn't help.
So I thought: this rhythm is like the rhythm of a slow-moving train.
Then I was on a train in Zimbabwe heading for Victoria Falls,
massive boulders outside the windows, monkeys climbing,
my body swaying, abuzz with wonder. Not alone. Then I felt
the loss. And now I am up again, writing,
trying to stop the train. Outside, jagged lines of lightning
flash against the flat black pines.

Impossible

I have walked two miles into human silence
which is not silent—pig frogs make their low groan
and insects buzz, whirr, vibrate, click. I move
through a world of cypress, epiphyte, fern,
butterflies at my legs. Some of these trees
have a huge girth. It would take three of me
with outstretched arms to encircle this one—
impossible embrace.

At the lettuce lake, an alligator floats
in green ruffles, his back strewn with a bright confetti,
pollen and small leaves—reptile in a Latin party dress.
I stare at this absurdity. The pileated woodpecker bangs
the pickaxe of his head against dead cypress.

Lobelia

In bright sunlight
this small spot of color

blue—arrests me

brings me to my knees
in complex grasses—

lavender lips
gland-tipped teeth
narcotic sap.

Earlier I saw a picture
said to myself

when I see this one
I will know it.

I press the hard-edged stem,
its slightly sticky fur.

Some old untamed attraction stirs.

Alligators in May

From the sawgrasses, the pond apples, the willow islands
and buttonbushes, from everywhere the water has risen, I hear
the guttural sounds begin, and then (I've heard about this, wanted it)
the gator's bellow. It repeats.

A louder bellow answers and another and... a low, choral thunder
speaks from the reeds—priests of the slough, monks growling
their prayers, their warnings, slow rhythm of the slough's breath,
throat song of these Everglades. Was it in a place like this

that ancient Tibetan monks first learned
how resonance evokes a spirit's
tender alertness? These are the gators'
mating calls. An irony? A lesson? A rebuke

for something we've forgotten—
tenderness a rumbling thunder of the body,
out of the throat, the spirit awake, trembling
in a clear water, wind bending the reeds.

Something that Lives

Somewhere deep in genetic memory
I know that this is what the world
should look like—prairie and sky.

On the African savannahs
I felt at home, not knowing
why. Even this wind

of which I am so inexplicably
fond, this sun lowering toward
the horizon, hot on my cheek,

wide wingspans turning over me,
familiar in some mysterious way.

Something that lives in this body
does not live in time. I am almost

but not quite, never quite, grasping.

A Stand of Old Slash Pine

Roots tendriled
into every acid-
eaten pock

every limestone
cleft and pore,
the narrow pines

lean
in wind
and sigh.

Sap rises
meager
a dark stain,

makes
a thin tight line
called growth.

After Fire

Not far from here, a thin skin of soil intact, this underbone
of limestone—ragged, pitted, is easily forgotten. Here

one must walk on it, hear the sound, every step crunch and cinder,
fragile stone, new ash, earth reshaping minutely with every pressure.

Blackened trunks of pines hold up their high green crowns, hold tight
to a pithy interior. I walk deeper in, where the understory has opened.

Drawn to the center of this burn, sun on my neck, I feel myself glowing
I crouch. Just another burned coontie, tuberous roots knotted in crevic

seeking any bit of moisture, needing the blaze, the charring back.
From this, the long new leaf unfurls.

Lubbers Mating

They wear the colors of caution and danger—yellow, red,
black—spew a toxic foam. The frog that swallows one
spits it back. But these unappealing hoppers, bellies full
of beauty berry and swamp lily, love with abandon.
They're doing it now all over the place

in the groundsel, the willows, the wild coffee,
on the muscular roots of the strangler fig,
in the morning glories, the gumbo limbo.
Before I saw them I heard them: *what's that sound?*

They vibrate, their red wings whirr, exoskeletons
click and rub, and this brave intensity, this exhibition
is not brief. Trusting their colors they risk the shadow,
the swoop, the beak's impalement

and something in me remembers, click and thrum,
dances, leggy, awkward, to castanets of the wild scrub.

Rangers of the Everglades

These are people who love the green
watery, actual world teeming
with fishes and birds and furry things,

things rooted and reaching toward sky,
blossoming and seeding, needling
and coning. They love the dirt. The mud.

They walk us along sloughs, naming:
great blue heron, little blue heron, egret,
ibis, red shouldered hawk. They tell us

how alligators love and how the anhinga
feed their young. They teach us
the patience of the wood stork, stirring

ooze with a pink foot, the reticence
of the bittern hiding in sawgrass.
They teach us *river*—not *swamp*,

wide river of grass flowing down the slow
incline of Florida—feeding, sustaining
except where humans interfere. Yes, us.

These rangers receive our questions, heavy
with ignorance, as though they were blessings.
They are glad we have come. They want *us*

to learn to name the world, too: otter,
alligator, spatterdock, gallinule,
osprey, cormorant, pond apple, gar.

That Yellow Fuzzy-Looking Stuff in the Water

Day after day I saw it, murky and unappealing,
floating and sinking everywhere, some sort of
algae I assumed. Did it belong here?
My ignorance is always blossoming.

Finally I took some in my fingers—
soft, spongy, not the slime I expected.
I've learned its name: *periphyton.*

Without this furry weave of organisms
making oxygen, making marl,
feeding the larvae of salamanders,
feeding the apple snails
that feed the snail kites
safekeeping eggs of a multitude of mothers
from the dry season to the wet season

everything here risks death—
even the armor plated gator
swallowing otters, turtles, birds
that feed on fish
that feed on the invisible

that depends upon
these soft ropes curling on water,
furry clumps hugging stems and blades,
this yellowy bottom fluff,
fresh smelling spongy stuff—
alive and alive and alive!

Season of Pond Apples

In the slough's orchards, alligators wait
for fat apples to fall—each a clean, hard splash.

Just then I heard a splash and now a gator, head thrust up,
jaws working, pink of his mouth visible, swallows.

Sometimes they squabble over these delicacies
that taste to us (or so I'm told) like turpentine.

I want to know for myself what that apple tastes like.
I've leaned over rails, bent branches, tried to reach one that's ripe.

Another splash. The gator in front of me gathers his legs,
swings the tail, moves with visible purpose.

Behind the leaves I hear his sloshy chomping.

This Bird

I'm glad to have
a name for it now

bird that flaps hard
against wind

climbs high, hangs
then folds its wings

dives

flings the soft arrow
of itself— *kestral*
to bedrock.

        This is the lucky
        dance of love—

at the last moment
spreading its wings.

Opossum Hand

—After Brian Call's photograph

All my life I have seen them—shy, hurrying
in their slow-hurry way
shunning company and light

grey mound of fur with bare tail, leaving.
Now this pink tinge of tapered claw,
these silver crescents of hair,

small hand, palm open, private
fleshy paleness I want to touch,
fingerprint brushing fingerprint—intimate,

tender. Grass luminescent, a loose pattern
behind the hand. Behind the pattern, darkness.

Disappearance

—After Brian Call's photograph, *Road-Killed American Bittern*

In these feathers a dry season, the colors of light
at dawn and evening, autumn and winter reeds—
whites, ambers, dark browns almost black,
textures like brush stroke, rhythms of curve,
soft light emanating from quills.
In the reeds, this is camouflage.

"You can't see it unless it moves," he tells me.
I cannot find it—shy bird hiding, lifting her head,
swaying in rhythm as winds bend the grasses,
this bird "just plain disappears."

Three days now I've been peering into the reeds.
I see only reeds camouflaged as bittern.

Softshell Turtle

The little blue heron steps
slowly, deliberately

her casual eye on me
and mine on her
till caution urges

and she lifts, flies
across the borrow pit.

In the space she vacates
the softshell turtle browses,
investigates with her pointy nose,

unhurried, in a turtle way
attentive, looking for something

sometimes toward me
sometimes away.

Whisperers

I appreciate them—those who whisper here, respecting
this wind, the way it prays. They walk expectant, gasp
softly at each illumination, each blessing of bird nest,
alligator or orchid. Pig frogs intone from the willows.

There is something we forget—and then
in a place like this we recognize
the turtle's nest of broken eggs
the heron's patience at an edge.

I'm glad for these final hours of light,
late setting of the sun, these whisperers,
this knowledge, this love
that will not abandon me.

Notes from a Marine Biologist's Daughter

My mother loves the salty mud of estuaries,
has no need of charts to know what time
low tide will come. She lives
by an arithmetic of moon,
calculates emergences of mud,

waits for all that crawls there, lays eggs,
buries itself in the shallow edges
of streamlets and pools. She digs
for *chaetopterus*, yellow and orange
worms that look like lace.

She leads me where *renilla* bloom
purple and white colonial lives,
where brittle stars, like moss,
cling to stone. She knows
where the sea horse wraps its tail
and the unseen lives of plankton.

My mother walks and sinks into an ooze,
centuries of organisms ground
to pasty darkness. The sun
burns at her shoulders
in its slow passage across the sky.
Light waves like pincers
in her mud-dark hair.

What Is this Frenzy of Naming?

Every day I go out with guides and charts,
checking undersides of leaves,
subtleties of feather, splotches on bark.
I want to know the names,
be able to say

good morning buttonbush,
good morning glossy ibis,
good morning gumbo limbo

as though by naming
I might claim an intimacy.

Intimacy requires more.
Intimacy is slow. It knows

not only what's here but what has been
and what is forming in the bud. For that
I must stay, know the subtle

rhythms of a year—what comes and goes
and comes again, sound of it, color of it,
shape and smell, sting and flower, how the tangle

thickens then recedes,
where waters move,
what burns. Now, the early sun

spreads over sawgrass. Dew dries. Water brightens.
One great blue heron arrives at the usual place.
All day he will stand there.

Taking in the Everglades

First I took in expanses of sawgrass bending in wind.
Then I fingered the sharp teeth that give it its name.

Yesterday at a shallow edge, I found tangles, strands
of small leaves, green flowerets. I pinched
and rubbed, breathed a lemony complex scent,
asked a ranger for its name: *lemon bacopa.* Edible.

Today I wade in, gather a handful of scented clusters,
open dark bread, place a layer of leaves over cheese,
make literal what I have whispered to myself—
I'm taking it into me, taking it in—pungent kick
to the familiar, lemon bite on my tongue.

On the Inundated Limestone Prairie

This is what I wanted—to stand in the middle of it. Marianne Moore
was right. I admire but do not own her detachment. In clear water
a foot deep, I am surrounded by ragged limestone forms, sinkholes
and pinnacles, entrances to passageways of fish. Gambusia swim

among the subtle colors and around my ankles, taking me into
the inundated Everglades. I, too,
make sustenance of water and light. Just over the edge

of my small precipice, softly furred gardens submerge and float,
stems intertwining—bladderwort, bacopa, musky mint, milkweed vine,
everything fuzzed with periphyton—blades, leaves, flowerettes
and the limestone, slippery, on which I stand.

Mother Collecting Marine Specimens

She poles the skiff from sunlight
into the drawbridge shadow, eases
against a piling, its muddy shapes
exposed by lowering tide.

In a cave-like cool, she nudges
grey clusters, crusty forms.
She scrapes, selects,
lays silty bits and clumps
in a bucket of clear water.

Intent, she peers and plucks.
A streak of blood appears on her thumb.
She doesn't notice. She never does.
I slide a finger over creosote blisters,
hear them pop, feel them flatten,
then stare into the realm of the underbridge—
great toothy gears, twisted cables.

Above our boat, the whirr of tires.
No one knows we're under here
or thinks of these barnacles,
their hair-like legs kicking
just below the water line.
Bells begin to clang, the hum
ceases, the bridge shudders,
its teeth begin to grind.

When we reenter brightness
and the ordinary pitch of traffic,

I lean to look in Mother's bucket:
green stones, yellow trees,
purple stars, an orange flame.

Mother in Water

"Did you see
how she stared and trembled?
If I ever get like that
I want you to row me
beyond the breakers,
push me over.
I mean it. Promise."

Sometimes I see us
in a small white boat.
At the bow, she sits,
back erect,
facing forward.
Her head jerks lightly.
I row. My arms ache,
eyes sting.
Behind us, land
flattens to a line.

Before she was twelve
she knew these waters,
poled alone
in a wooden skiff
through the winding maze
of slough and marsh,
channel and sandbar;
she'd beach the boat,
take off her shirt and swim.

Only water now. Water.

How easily, quietly
it opens. Just
beneath the surface
I see her gliding
gills opening
expanding like sponges
waving like feathers.
A flash of silver
darts into the green.

Touch Feeding

In the Everglades, what I want to touch:
soft down of the young anhinga's S-curved neck
shiny leather of the gator's black back
fleshy palm of the opossum

smooth haunch of the yellow panther
wrinkled neck of the soft-shell turtle
underwing where the ibis preens
tongue of the great blue heron

the touch-feeding wood stork's pink feet
stirring, stirring till the small fish darts
and the sensitive beak, quickest motion
in nature—snaps shut.

Transcendent
—After Brian Call's *Road-Killed Purple Gallinule*

This is a bird. This garden of fine, hair-like greens
and blues, these delicate crossings and interlacings,
this jeweled seaweed swaying. This is a bird
so close I have never seen a bird so close.

This is a photograph. The photographer stood
in a dark road, bent over the dead bird, laid upon it
a beam of light, paid tribute with his lens, his eye,
then lifted it into its final motion, gave it
gently to the earth. This is a photograph.

I look at it and weep and soar I am green I am
blue I am waving—a wing, a seaweed thing, I fly.

In this Life

What I want is for something fine
to happen inside my body
and to make of that something a form
that when the body is gone

will be left behind
with that fine something encoded
in it so that somebody else
happening on it, will find

something fine happening inside
their body, and they will make of that
something, something fine.

V

Key West after a Month in the Everglades

Streets full of people in shorts, my jeans are wrong. I am hot.
I am in another country, awkward in simple negotiations.
At the hotel I couldn't remember my departure date.
Twice I've set off the car alarm.

Key West today has no appeal for me—except these chickens,
three roosters and a hen under the gumbo limbo, scratching dirt.
I watch, wonder what's happening now at the Anhinga Trail.
Is that gangly pile of baby gators sunning in the spatterdock?
At this time of day, the gator with the wounded tail, pink
flesh protruding through leather, stretches under the willows.
In the clear stream that flows from the slough,
long quiet gar hover in shadows, ancient
armor under their thin-stretched skins.

Loss of Innocence, Krome Avenue & Hwy 41

In this landscape of dikes, locks, levees,
billboards—*Everglades Safari Here!*
one canal parallels the road where an animal
is flattened beyond recognition.

For weeks now I have been learning to read
the River of Grass and now at this perimeter,
I am losing my innocence. A "prettiness"
I once loved, water hyacinth and cattail,
spells stagnation. The softness of Australian pine,
bright red berries of Brazilian pepper—exotic
escapees, threats to complexity—choke out natives.

Odd this feeling of homesickness
(I don't know what else to call it)
nervous desire to get back in the park
where however altered, however threatened,
something whole teaches me how to live.

Road-Killed Black Racer

—After Brian Call's photograph

Something in me recoils from the very shape—
the bent stick, the curling bit of rope.

How will I learn to love this black racer—
faster than a rattler, faster
than the coral snake, the rat snake, the hognose,
faster than the copperhead, the ringneck.

Not fast enough. Its skin
separates from its body, its muscle
turns to dust, shrinks
to the skeletal outline.

I could learn to love it as color, yes, as pattern,
but it's the very life I must love,
the animating force, its terrifying motion.

My culture's stories of evil and betrayal
work against me. What would the Miccosukee say?
Where would they tell me this serpent's spirit is?

What might they teach me of the Snake Dance,
taking the sinuous motion into my own body,
making me the thing despised,
the thing I must learn to love.

Sunday Morning

Vultures report to work.'
No holidays for them.
What must be done must be done.
Every day.

A crew of them gathers
near the edge of the road
at the raccoon's body.

They pace, assess. Then each
with his own strong muscle
punches in.

Wilderness

From a wide domesticated expanse—
neatly tame and furrowed rows,
tomatoes, beans, obedient fields,

this remnant of wildness rises.
Cross over a boundary and there you are
in some other dimension of the self—
a lush unfettered flourishing.

Then you know
what the plow turns under
what the traffic kills.

Road-Killed American Alligator

—After Brian Call's photograph

In this photo exhibit that amazes me
(I return day after day)
I try not to look at this photograph.

I glance, walk by, but it drags itself
through the sawgrass and piney woods,
follows me home. Last night when I lay down

it was there—the body badly torn, the eye
ripped from its socket with a nest of bloody
tissue, jaw broken completely,

the long body empty of breath, deflated.
Spilling from the torn stomach, carapaces,
claws—whole ragged crustaceans.

Alligator Hand

—After Brian Call's photograph *Alligator Foot*

This is the forefoot—as easily called
an arm, a hand. I see that soft bend
at the wrist, feel my own wrist bending.

All our grasping comes to this—
the bluish wrist, the blue-black hand,
curved nails on a brown leaf.

Something from the darkness comes too fast.

Lightning at Paradise Key

If ever I were to be struck by lightning I would want it to be here
on just such an early evening in the season of storms—
clouds, water, buttonbush blossoms luminous,
this sudden wind speaking in fluttering tongues.

Out on the gulf a depression whirls, flings trails of cloud
over these Everglades. And suddenly the sky is drained of light,
and suddenly the key is flashing. The gator does not move.
I step closer, bend down in the wind and stare,
his dark world of an eye uncovered, looking straight at me now.

El Laguno del Espiritu Santo

Not knowing what to do
with the map of South Florida,

impenetrable expanses of water and blades
that were not gold, not silver, not anything

valuable, those Spaniards dismissed it,
named it for the Holy Spirit, moved on.

Order stirs now in the sawgrass prairie wind.
A wood stork sails its cross over the slough.

An anhinga dives, then spreads its wings to dry.
The gator holds the turtle on his tongue.

VI

Alligator Efficiency

Everything, everything gets digested—fur, teeth, bones, feathers,
the turtle's shell, the armadillo's armor. Digestion is what they do,
what they do all day long—in the sun if its cool, in the shade
if it's hot. The next meal will not be an issue for weeks.

The ibis know. Unconcerned, they pace nearby, stir mud.
One flutters to a gator's back, stretches, shakes.
It's these birds who need the constant intake.
Theirs is not the luxury of unhurried, deliberate digest.

I admire the alligator's efficiency of slow—taking in,
taking in completely, making the intake part of the body,
leaving behind something small. Something chalky. Fine.

After the Burn

Remnant flames still gnaw at the coontie root,
ride the silver fallen trunk, make an understory of smoke.

For years, every fire that dropped from the sky was a call
to suppression. Finally we learned the necessity of burning.

After fire comes something new, something wild
with a new lush. I feel the air here quivering.

Tomorrow I can walk this ash. Today, now, it is too hot
and there is something private about this moment between

the burn and the new. I keep my edge, breathe smoke.
Birds wait in the sighing crowns.

Waiting at Taylor Slough

In the shush of willow,
among the quiet epiphytes

a single anhinga
spreads its pattern.

When will it happen?
When will I arrive and find
the season changed again

slough busy
with winged divers,
pond apple branches
silvering with guano.

In dense vegetation
I see the opening,
a gator-slide,

lean, peer in, gasp lightly
at the teeth, the truth, the eyes.

Dragonfly

I've been sitting here so still, so long.
Always into stillness a small miracle comes.
I am watching a dragonfly breathe. In the brown body
under cellophane wings, its rhythm is not unlike my own.

Now she lifts, flies from the rail, but surprises me,
circles back to the corner to my page
where I can see the left rear wing—badly torn,
left front also damaged.

Wings on the right appear perfect
until I lean closer, see the ragged edges.
Not one of these wings is perfect.
Yet—she flies.

At Season's End, Singing to the Alligator

I was prepared to arrive at the slough and for the first time
find no gators there, but there was one swimming steadily
away from the boardwalk. I watched.

I began to sing to him (I don't know why), hum rather.
He slowed down. A coincidence probably. I kept humming.
He stopped, turned sideways, looked at me.

I came then as close to holding my breath
as one can while humming.

He began to submerge (felt safer that way, I suppose)
but did not submerge completely. I hummed.

Slowly, he swam toward me
stopped directly beneath me
hung in the water the way they do
legs dangling, listening.
(Be skeptical if you will.
I know that gator was listening.)

We stayed that way a long time,
I leaning over the rail humming,
he looking up at me, attentive—
until he folded his legs to his body,
waved that muscled tail and left me

alone, dizzy with inexplicable joy.

Pahayokee

I lay a long time in a band of light,
in the rhythm of cicada, whirr of gnats,
clouds creeping over cypress
dragging their shadows through sawgrass.

This is the way the world is when we're not there—
insects whirling, the egret's intermittent croak.
How long, I wondered, would I have to stay
before... what? What am I wanting?

Brightness withdraws. A pale light settles
on the prairie, on cypress, on the blue dragonfly,
its veined wings. It will live a few more days.

I am inconsequential here.
I am inconsequential everywhere,
but here I have no illusions.

Whatever dies dies.
What gets devoured gets devoured.
Waters rise and fall, clouds move,
the buzzing profusion continues.

Earlier I went to look at wildflowers, stumbled on bones—
one was wing-like, flipper-like, perhaps a shoulder blade.
What would my shoulder blade look like
if it sprouted a wing?
One bone curved like the S of a violin's body. It sang.

Reclamation

This is how we heal the earth—one dry acre at a time scraped bare,
an invasive tangle of scrub uprooted, hauled away in monstrous trucks,
the earth itself extracted, its bad seed, the exotic berry.

The rainy season comes. Water collects in shallow calcium pools.
I wade into a rising tide of grasses, sedge and wildflower.
Here and as far as I can see this dry sternum becomes
wetland again. It knows how. Nobody planted anything here.

I keep coming back to learn from this limestone
reclaiming colors and subtle motions, becoming a place
for deer and butterflies. And me. Mice, too, somewhere,
and snakes that follow them into the garden of hungers.

Old Resin

I can never keep them completely separate,
blessings and the French *blessures*.
What's the difference anyway, *blessing* and *wound*.
Think of the stigmata, the holy blood.
I walk among these trees and every one
with any age shows signs. All are blessed.
Some marked by a black char
have been struck by lightning, some torn by storm.

What caused this pine's deep gash, I wonder,
and how long ago. Bark ripped away,
heartwood gouged, beetles moved in,
ants came, and then the woodpeckers probing,
every one of them glad. Streams of balming resin poured
and thick lips formed around the busy wound.

Do not confuse this balm with sap, clear fluid carrying
the business of life, supporting growth, the upward reach.
Resin's only purpose is the wound, its healing.
No wonder we prize the amber jewel's light,
the tender resonance of rosin on the bow.
Gingerly, I reach and touch
the old resin, hard and red.

Blood Meal

I eat of lemon bacopa.
The mosquito drinks my blood.

My eating is ritual.
Her eating is life.

No difference.
We do what we must.

She pollinates the orchid,
lays her eggs.

I look for myself
blooming in the branches.

Animalia

Alligator—During the dry season in Everglades National Park, alligators congregate at small bodies of water, including near the Anhinga Trail where they can be observed at close range, sunning or swimming. In their native habitat and natural condition, alligators do not see humans as prey and are not dangerous unless provoked. They become dangerous when they have been actively or passively fed by humans.

Anhinga—A large water bird that dives and swims underwater, the anhinga spears fish with its sharp beak and then flips the fish into the air, catches and swallows it whole, head first. The anhinga can often be seen standing on a branch near water, its wings spread wide, drying or thermoregulating. When it swims just beneath the surface, its tail feathers spread like an elegant fan.

Bittern—Solitary, shy and stealthy, this large wading bird is seldom seen. It hides by standing in tall vegetation, raising its long neck, pointing its bill skyward and standing perfectly still or, if there is wind, waving with the vegetation.

Black Racer—I have learned to love the black racer, slender, graceful and quick, on the ground or twining through small trees and scrub. Though mostly black, it has a white chin, clearly visible when it lifts its head. It is not venomous, but if you try to pick it up, it can be feisty and bite.

Egret—The great egret was hunted to near extinction during the late 19th and 20th centuries when its beautiful white feathers (especially mating plumes) were all the rage in fashion and an ounce of feather was worth more than an ounce of gold. Efforts of the early Audubon Society resulted in the outlawing of the feather trade, but populations have never fully recovered.

Gambusia—Also known as mosquito fish, gambusia feed upon mosquito larvae. These small fish at the bottom of the food web help to sustain a delicate balance and are, themselves, food for larger fishes.

Gar—The Florida gar has always reminded me of a giraffe, with its spotted pattern, its long nose. This ancient fish has armored plates under its skin and an air bladder which enables it to breathe air for limited amounts of time during a severe drydown.

Great Blue Heron—Largest of the herons of south Florida, the great blue heron hunts small fish, frogs, and snakes. Typically, it stands in shallow water, motionless, for long periods of time, awaiting its prey.

Ibis—These large wading birds probe mud and sometimes dirt of the shore with their long, curved beaks, searching for crayfish and insects. The white ibis has an orange beak. The glossy ibis is darkly iridescent and has a dark beak.

Kestrel—The American Kestrel is a small falcon with distinctive reddish, blue, and yellow markings. These birds are smaller in Florida than in the north.

Lubber—Colorful lubber grasshoppers prefer low moist areas with an overstory, and they are abundant in the Everglades. At certain times of year, there are so many of them on the first section of the Anhinga Trail that it takes real effort not to step on one.

Panther—The Florida Panther is the official state mammal of Florida. This shy, tawny yellow panther is a seriously endangered subspecies of the western cougar. As destruction of habitat progresses, its outlook is dim, in spite of ongoing research and dedicated preservation efforts. Most panther deaths occur on the highway at night.

Pied-billed Grebe—This small water bird submerges when disturbed and can stay underwater for such a long time that it has been sometimes been called "hell-diver."

Pig Frog—After the bullfrog, this is the largest Florida frog. The tympanum of the male is larger than its eye; the female's tympanum is a little smaller but highly visible. In the Everglades, the loud bass frog in the chorus or the lone deeply resonant voice from the sawgrass prairie is usually the pig frog.

Purple Gallinule—The jewel-like blues and greens of this bird, the bright red on its beak and its yellow legs, make this one of the brightest birds in the Everglades. Its long toes allow it to walk lightly from lily pad to lily pad.

Python—Pythons are not native to south Florida, but in recent years they have been sighted with increasing frequency. In spite of efforts to eradicate them, they are now well established and breeding in Everglades National Park. Pythons released from captivity were the original source of this population. No one knows what the long-term effect will be. Research is underway.

Red Shouldered Hawk—The distinctive high-pitched call (*keeyuur, keeyuur*) is a common sound in south Florida. These beautiful hawks hunt from perches, preferring to perch along forest edges or in a tall tree at the edge of a prairie. Red shouldered hawks are one of the best snake-hunting hawks in the south.

Softshell Turtle—The long neck and slender pointy nose of the Florida softshell turtle make it a great snorkeler. Its leathery shell is wide and much flatter than most turtles. Its beak is sharp and its jaws are powerful—beware. I have often seen this turtle swimming alongside the Anhinga Trail at Taylor Slough and have sometimes seen females laying eggs in sand near the water's edge.

Vulture—The turkey vulture has a red head, a white edge along the trailing wing, and flies with its wings in a V shape. The black vulture has a gray head, white wing tips, and flies with its wings stretched straight. Both vultures kettle above the Everglades in high spirals, looking for prey.

Wood stork—This large endangered bird is highly dependent for its survival upon timing, quantity, and quality of water in the wetlands. If water cycles are disrupted, wood storks may go a whole season without reproducing. Genetic testing has revealed that the wood stork is related to the vulture, with whom it shares a featherless head.

Love the animals, love the plants, love everything.
—Fyodor Dostoyevsky

Botanica

Bladderwort—This floating aquatic plant is carnivorous. It has many small bladder-like structures with triggers that are activated by the presence of tiny prey. The trigger snaps the trap, and the organism is caught and digested. This hungry plant puts forth diminutive, elegant yellow or lavender flowers.

Brazillian Pepper—Its red berries attractive, this invasive exotic plant was originally imported for landscaping. It has escaped into the wild and aggressively taken over thousands of acres in south Florida, displacing native plants and animals, destroying productive habitat.

Buttonbush—Its tiny fragrant flowers, emerging from a central ball, are attractive to bees and butterflies. The Miccosukee Indian word for buttonbush means "alligator shader." It blooms March through August.

Cattail—Although cattails are native to Florida, they overgrow in areas where high nutrient runoff has created abnormal conditions. Heavy concentrations of cattail are, therefore, a signal of water degradation.

Coontie—Looking fern-like, the coontie is actually a cycad, the only cycad native to Florida. These ancient plants were on the planet at the time of the dinosaurs and are well adapted to cycles of wet and dry as well as to fire. When the fronds are burned to the ground, the thick fist of underground root very quickly sends up new green shoots.

Epiphyte—Commonly known as airplants, epiphytes of the Everglades include many species of orchids and colorful bromeliads. These use their host trees for structure only and are not parasitic. They absorb water and nutrients from the air. The famous and familiar southern Spanish moss is an epiphyte.

Gumbo Limbo—The smooth bark of the gumbo limbo peels off in thin ragged layers. This bark is often quite red, and the tree has gained the nickname of "tourist tree" because it is red and peeling. The strong wood was once preferred for making carousel horses. The Gumbo Limbo Trail in Everglades National Park gives a close-up look at many of these trees.

Lemon Bacopa—Crush a few leaves of lemon bacopa and you will know from the scent where it gets its name. Often, these aquatic plants grow and float together, making a garden of small leaves and diminutive blue flowers.

Lobelia—The Glades Lobelia, with its purple-blue flowers, is one of several lobelias growing in wetland areas. It is attractive to hummingbirds but poisonous to humans.

Pond Apple—The pond apple's bell-shaped flowers precede the apple that gives it its name. At the Anhinga Trail and elsewhere, anhinga often use pond apple trees as nesting sites.

Sawgrass—The famous sawgrasses of the Everglades are not grasses at all; they are sedges. *Sedges have edges.* If you feel a sawgrass blade, be careful. Running your finger up to the tip will be no problem, but if you try to follow the edge in the opposite direction, you will discover the serrated edges that cut like a saw.

Slash Pine—The tall slender slash pines of the Everglades pinelands are fully adapted to the cycles of wet and dry, and they need periodic fire. Slow growing, their wood is dense. Very slender pines may be quite old.

Spatterdock—Broad, heart-shaped leaves float on the water like lily pads; purple gallinules use them as stepping stones. The yellow fist of flower looks like a bud about to open, but that's as open as it gets.

Swamp Lily—This large, star-like flower of the wetlands, blooming in sawgrass prairies, is not a true lily. Also known as String Lily, it is a relative of the amaryllis. It serves as a larval food plant for Monarch and Queen butterflies and is a favorite food of Lubber grasshoppers.

The gumbo limbo swoons in the arms of the oak.
—Lola Haskins

The Poet

Anne McCrary Sullivan's poems have appeared in a number of literary journals and anthologies, including *the Marlboro Review, Fourth River, Earth's Daughters, Tar River Poetry, The Caribbean Writer, The Gettysburg Review,* and *The Southern Review.* She has an M.F.A in Poetry from Warren Wilson College and a Ph.D. in English Education from the University of Florida. *Ecology II: Throat Song from The Everglades* is her first full-length collection. She is a Florida Master Naturalist who lives, writes, explores and teaches in southwest Florida.

The Photographer

Brian F. Call's passionate eye records the flora, fauna, geology and hydrology of southwest Florida. His work has appeared in print venues including *Nature's Best Magazine, Nature Photographer, National Wildlife* and *Miami Monthly,* as well as in other media, including PBS programming. He exhibits widely in Florida and beyond. Brian is deeply committed to environmental issues and to the preservation of natural South Florida. He has a fine arts degree from Montserrat College of Art.

Wilderness, to me, is a spiritual necessity.
—Clyde Butcher

Made in United States
Orlando, FL
05 February 2022

14402966R20064